LIFE & UNDEAD

BOOK OF ELEMENTS

GROSSET & DUNLAP
Published by the Penguin Group
Penguin Group (USA) LLC, 375 Hudson Street, New York, New York 10014, USA

USA | Canada | UK | Ireland | Australia | New Zealand | India | South Africa | China

penguin.com
A Penguin Random House Company

Written by Barry Hutchison

Copyright © 2014 by Activision Publishing, Inc. Skylanders Universe is a trademark and Activision is a registered trademark of
Activision Publishing, Inc. Published by Grosset & Dunlap, a division of Penguin Young Readers Group, 345 Hudson Street,
New York, New York 10014. GROSSET & DUNLAP is a trademark of Penguin Group (USA) LLC. Printed in the USA.

ISBN 978-0-448-48046-6   10 9 8 7 6 5 4 3 2 1

LIFE & UNDEAD

BOOK OF ELEMENTS

GROSSET&DUNLAP
An Imprint of Penguin Group (USA) LLC

CONTENTS

LIFE

UNDEAD

WELCOME!
FROM FLYNN AND HUGO

Well, hey, there! So you want to know about the Life and Undead Elements, do you? You've come to the right guy. I know pretty much everything there is to know about . . . well, everything! So strap yourselves in and put on your crash helmets. It's going to be one exciting ride!

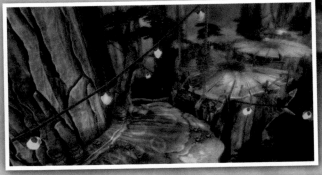

Forgive my overexcitable colleague. Safety equipment will not be necessary. All you need to learn about the Life and Undead Elements are a knowledgeable guide and an inquisitive mind. Oh, and possibly a light snack. I can provide the first of those three. If you can provide the other two, we'll be in business.

WHERE DOES LIFE COME FROM?

There is no avoiding the Life Element. It exists all around us. You'll find Life everywhere (except at one of Hugo's parties —Flynn). It is the Element that ensures Skylands maintains its natural balance.

From the tiniest seed to the tallest tree, from the smallest grub to the largest land whale, Skylands teems with Life. Those Skylanders who harness the Life element are at one with the plants, the trees and the very soil itself. This grants them incredible abilities to use in the fight against Kaos and his minions. It also means that some of them are jolly good at gardening.

Life is there in the deepest depths of the ocean. It survives in the fiery hearts of volcanoes. Even in the most inhospitable of conditions, Life carries on, and this makes it a very powerful Element indeed.

ONE TRIP TO SKYLANDS AND YOU'LL NEVER LOOK AT TREES IN THE SAME WAY AGAIN!

ᐦO NOT FEEᐦ THE TROLLS

Like most Elements, Life has suffered many times at the hands of Kaos and his minions. Trolls in particular seem to go out of their way to damage the natural balance of things.

Though they are clumsy buffoons, trolls are also engineering types by nature, and sadly they have polluted the environment more than any other species in Skylands. Their factories belch out thick, oily smoke, their oil drills chew up the ground, and the air turns a nasty shade of yellowish green every time they break wind (or so I've been told).

The biggest problem is their inventions, which are usually designed to cause immense harm to the natural world. Even when they're designed for other purposes, they normally end up causing immense harm to the natural world anyway. Especially when they explode.

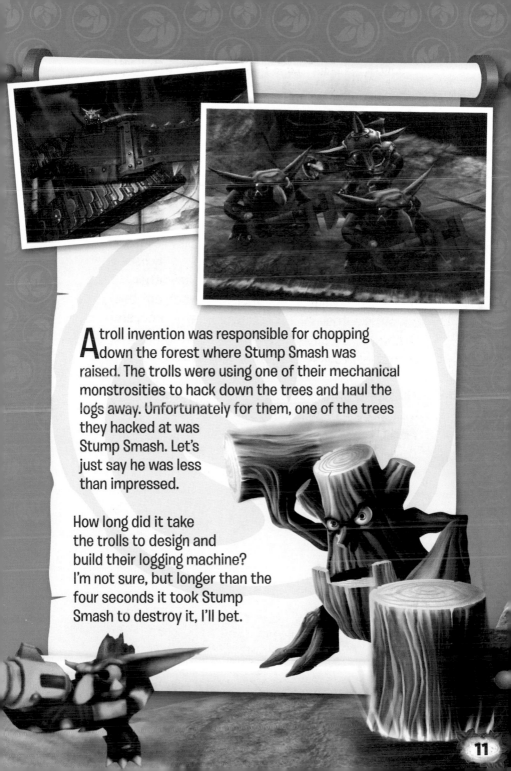

A troll invention was responsible for chopping down the forest where Stump Smash was raised. The trolls were using one of their mechanical monstrosities to hack down the trees and haul the logs away. Unfortunately for them, one of the trees they hacked at was Stump Smash. Let's just say he was less than impressed.

How long did it take the trolls to design and build their logging machine? I'm not sure, but longer than the four seconds it took Stump Smash to destroy it, I'll bet.

NATURE BITES BACK

Far back in the mists of time, many centuries before I was even born (wow, that is a long time ago—Flynn), a tall tree dominated the Skylands landscape. It stood at the heart of a lush forest, towering over the trees around it. It was peaceful. It was happy. Or as happy as a tree can be, at least. I doubt it was cracking jokes or anything.

Everything changed when the ancient civilization known as the Arkeyans built a war factory in the shadows of the forest. As they constructed their weapons, they were unwittingly polluting the area around the factory. Tech and Magic waste seeped into the forest, and was absorbed by the roots of this tall, majestic tree.

For many years the pollution soaked into the tree's roots and was carried to its highest branches. The toxins should have killed it, but instead something quite remarkable happened: the tree mutated. It sprouted mighty arms and powerful legs, and even grew a rather fetching pair of mossy underpants. Bellowing what would become his catchphrase—"Be Afraid of the Bark!"—the gigantic Tree Rex pulled himself free of the polluted soil, then promptly stomped the war-machine factory to pieces.

WHAT DID TREE REX WEAR TO THE SKYLANDS POOL PARTY?

SWIMMING TRUNKS!

Since that day, Tree Rex has dedicated his life to maintaining the natural balance of all things. If you're thinking of harming the environment, stop and look up. There may just be an enormous wooden foot about to squish you flat!

TREE REX

DID YOU KNOW?

For months, Tree Rex was bothered by a pounding headache that would keep him awake at night. It was only when Master Eon appeared in spirit form and took a closer look that he discovered a family of woodpeckers living inside the Giant's wooden skull. After the wise old Portal Master instructed Hugo to lure the birds out with a cookie on a piece of string, Tree Rex's headache vanished for good. Hooray!

FACT FILE

- Was once a tall, majestic tree cheerfully minding his own business
- Despite the rumors, counting his rings will not tell you his age
- His tree-trunk feet are perfect for stomping on enemies
- Can spray lethal laser blasts from his arm cannon

LIFE RATING

 **95%**

SHROOMBOOM

FACT FILE

- Born in a garden belonging to Kaos
- Uses his slingshot to devastating effect
- Can use his mushroom cap head to glide short distances
- A real *fungi* to be around (sorry, Flynn made me write that part)

DID YOU KNOW?

There are over 10,000 different species of mushroom in Skylands. Of those 10,000, Shroomboom is the only one to have dedicated his life to fighting the forces of evil. Many of the rest, to give them their due, go on to enjoy successful careers as ingredients in soups and stews, or toppings on pizzas.

67%

LIFE RATING

STUMP SMASH

FACT FILE

- Used to enjoy nothing more than a nice nap
- He and his entire forest were cut down by trolls
- His tree stump fists allow him to smash enemies big and small
- Can spit out spiny acorns— an attack that is both effective and disgusting

DID YOU KNOW?

Stump Smash used to love the sound of the wind whistling through his branches. He longs to make beautiful music again, but his mallet fists can make piano lessons tricky. Legend has it he can play a mean xylophone solo, though.

84%

LIFE RATING

16

ZOOK

FACT FILE

- Hails from a species known as the Bambazookers
- Stood in the mud for years —until he realized he could walk
- Wandered the forests seeking peace, harmony, and things to blow up
- Is the subject of several popular campfire songs

DID YOU KNOW?

The hand-carved tube Zook carries with him has many uses. Among other things it acts as a telescope, a musical instrument, and a place to store his lunch. It can also be used as a high-powered rocket launcher with which to fight his enemies— provided he remembers to take his sandwiches out first.

LIFE RATING

65%

STEALTH ELF

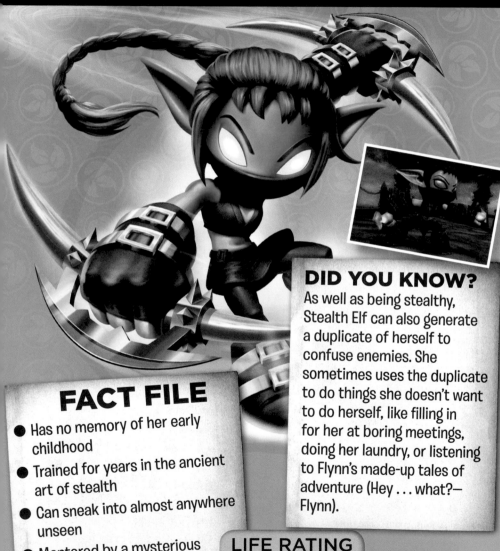

DID YOU KNOW?

As well as being stealthy, Stealth Elf can also generate a duplicate of herself to confuse enemies. She sometimes uses the duplicate to do things she doesn't want to do herself, like filling in for her at boring meetings, doing her laundry, or listening to Flynn's made-up tales of adventure (Hey . . . what?— Flynn).

FACT FILE

- Has no memory of her early childhood
- Trained for years in the ancient art of stealth
- Can sneak into almost anywhere unseen
- Mentored by a mysterious forest ninja

LIFE RATING

89%

CAMO

72%

LIFE RATING

FACT FILE

- Loves playing pranks
- Half dragon, half plant, hatched from the roots of the Tree of Life
- Can cause plants and foliage to grow at an incredible rate
- Once exploded a melon in Master Eon's confused, frightened face

DID YOU KNOW?

The peppers Camo can grow from his tail are among the hottest in all of Skylands. Only the Fire Skylander, Eruptor, has ever been able to eat a whole one. He appeared to suffer no lasting effects, but he did spend almost a week lying down in a darkened room afterward, and he hasn't been able to look at spicy food since.

SECRETS OF THE ELEMENTS:
LIFE

The Life Element flows through all living things, and there are plenty of living things to flow through on Skylands. There are thousands upon thousands of different species living here—and those are just the ones we know about.

LEGENDARY CREATURES

Experts—well, me, mostly—believe that there are many more living things waiting to be discovered around Skylands. Countless legends exist, telling of weird and wonderful creatures that may lurk in the shadowy forests. There are tales of living leaves and singing bushes, of flying elves and fishing gnomes. Are the legends true? Who knows? Only time will tell for sure.

THE TREE OF LIFE

The Tree of Life is ancient and sprawling, and almost as large as an entire woodland. It is inhabited by a race of rather lovely tree folk, but it is also home to nasties such as Corn Hornets, Life Spell Punks, and Blade Witches. The tree brims with Life energy, and when the Skylander Camo was born from its roots, some of that energy was transferred to him.

LIFE IMITATES LIFE

Skylanders aligned with the Life Element have many things in common. They are powerful against the Water Element, but less capable against the Undead. Their abilities help them create and grow new living things of their own—from plants and vines to animated dummies. And they also like the color green. A lot.

CALI'S HEROIC CHALLENGES

It's not all fun and games being a Skylander. Okay, so most of the time it is, but these guys never get to let down their guard. If they do, then—BOOM!—my gal Cali hits them with a challenge to keep them on their toes. If they have toes. Some of them don't.

MINEFIELD MISHAP

When Stealth Elf heard about the challenge my Cali had set her, she was almost offended by how easy it sounded. All she had to do was get through the fortress and find the Royal Scepter of Nort. Then Cali told her the fortress was full of trolls. There were dozens of landmines hidden underground, too. Oh, and she only had two and a half minutes to complete the challenge. Luckily, Stealth Elf was able to sneak past the trolls and dodge the mines. She reached the scepter just in time, but I doubt she'll ever call Cali's challenges "too easy" again!

S.A.B.R.I.N.A.

My Cali has a beautiful heart. The rest of her isn't bad, either, but it was her heart that led her to come up with Tree Rex's heroic challenge. We all know that geckos love to sing, right? They sing to their king. Constantly. Day and night. Anyway, this annoyed a pretty nasty sorceress named Sabrina, so she locked up those little guys and their king.

Tree Rex had to fight some real ugly brutes before he could smash open the cages and set the geckos free. Cali believes no one should be locked up for singing, but clearly she hadn't heard those little guys in action—they sounded even worse than Gill Grunt! Well, okay, no one sounds worse than Gill Grunt—but they came pretty close!

TREE REX'S ANTLERS ARE _TREE_-NORMOUS!

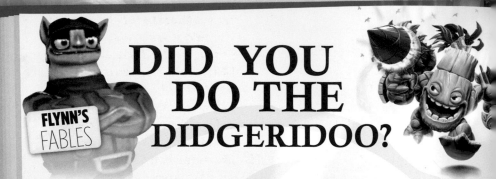

DID YOU DO THE DIDGERIDOO?

FLYNN'S FABLES

Zook just loves to get out there and explore the world. Hey, you would, too, if you'd spent most of your life standing in the same place! So when he's not needed to defend Skylands, he'll head off walking for days on end, finding new places and discovering new things.

One time he discovered more than he bargained for—Kaos's Dark Witch Minion. This evil double of Hex was up to no good, terrorizing a group of Molekin who happened to be in the wrong place at the wrong time. Our Bambazooker didn't like facing her magic head-on, so he hung back and took aim with his bamboo bazooka. But then—disaster! He realized he'd forgotten to take any ammunition with him. His bazooka was useless! He couldn't leave those poor Molekin at the mercy of Hex's double, though. One had already

been transformed into a slug, while two others had been given chicken heads and covered in feathers. The Zookster knew he had to stop her, but the Dark Witch Minion was way powerful.

wasn't there to see it either, but I'm told it was quite a sight. She stopped attacking the poor Molekin and clamped her hands over her ears. The Zookmeister turned up the volume, and soon the witch couldn't take it any more. She turned and fled, keeping her ears covered all the way.

Luckily, Zook had an idea. The Dark Witch is exactly like Hex, and if there's one thing Hex can't stand it's Zook's didgeridoo playing!

So, getting as close as he could, Zook put his bazooka to his lips and let fly with a blast of deafening didge. You should have seen that evil double's face! Well, I

With that nasty piece of work out of the way, Zook took the Molekin back to the real Hex, who agreed to change them back to their former selves. Hex had to admit that, even though she hated the sound of it, Zook's didgeridoo playing could sure come in handy at times!

ELEMENTAL GATES:
LIFE LOCATIONS

Dotted all over Skylands are incredible hidden areas that can only be accessed by Skylanders of certain Elements. Thanks to my years of research, I have been able to chart the locations of many of the gates encountered by the Life Skylanders during their adventure to rebuild the Core of Light . . .

STORMY STRONGHOLD

One of the first Life Elemental gates you'll encounter is in the Stormy Stronghold. There's nothing too challenging here—just a few Chompies really, which you'll take care of easily. Oh, and some Drow Spearmen. They're quite tricky, actually. And did I mention they're being protected by an Air Spell Punk? Well, perhaps it is quite tricky after all. After you take care of all the enemies in this area, head right, and you'll find the gate. There are some rock-pushing puzzles to solve on the other side, but nothing you can't handle, I'm sure!

HARD

ACCESS OF LOCATION

EASY

TROLL WAREHOUSE

You'll have to face some Rocket Imps to get to this Life Elemental gate, so it won't be easy. You know you're getting close when you find the minefield (be careful!)—the gate is just a little further along the path. In the new area, you'll find a number of locked doors and a number of keys. Using the keys in the correct order is the—er—key. (Sorry for saying the word *key* so much.)

HARD

ACCESS OF LOCATION

EASY

QUICKSILVER VAULT

You'll have a real battle on your hands before you reach this Elemental gate, I'm afraid. You'll find it in the Main Gate area, but the only way to reach it is to defeat numerous Arkeyan fighters—including an Ultron! Once you've taken care of business, a teleporter will appear, and it'll bring the Elemental gate with it. You'll need fast reactions and steady nerves to cross the floating platforms in the new area. Be careful out there.

HARD

ACCESS OF LOCATION

EASY

FOOD FRIGHT

FLYNN'S FABLES

Not a lot of people know this, but Ghost Roaster once had the chance to become a celebrity chef. He was offered a job touring and demonstrating his cooking skills in front of live audiences. As well as the fame, he was going to be given as many ghosts as he could eat—and that guy can eat a lot of ghosts!

The Roastmeister General only had to pass one audition and the job was his. Luckily for us (but not so luckily for Ghost Roaster), Camo offered to help out with the audition by providing all the ingredients. Maybe it was all the excitement of the audition, but Ghost Roaster didn't even get suspicious. Camo is well known for his pranks, but Ghost Roaster agreed that the little dragon could help.

Camo supplied all sorts of fruits and vegetables for the audition. It wasn't the sort of thing Ghost Roaster usually cooked up, but he still remembered enough from his days back in the mountains to know what to do.

But little Camo had other ideas. The audition started with a bang—literally! A carrot went *pop* in Ghost Roaster's hand. Still, Ghost Roaster carried on like a true pro. He was doing quite well until a cabbage exploded, showering him with shredded leaves and several confused caterpillars.

Anyone else would've given up then, but not Ghostie. He kept going, despite the laughter coming from Camo. Ghost Roaster reached for a chili pepper. Camo covered his ears and . . .

Needless to say, he didn't pass the audition. But that's okay—we think he's better off in the Skylanders, anyway! Being a celeb chef might be glamorous, but only Skylanders get the opportunity to kick Kaos's butt!

BOOM!

The pepper erupted, starting a massive chain reaction of exploding food. There was melon dripping from the ceiling and tomato oozing down every wall. Poor Ghost Roaster was coated from head to toe.

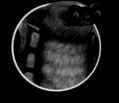

THE ANCIENT ART OF
STEALTH

Stealth Elf always had a knack for being sneaky, which was probably why she was chosen by the Forest Guardian to be trained in the ancient art of stealth. Thanks to her training, she can move silently across any surface, become invisible, and even make a decoy double of herself to keep enemies distracted.

She's a real danger with anything sharp, too. Give her a sword or knife and she can take out entire armies of enemies. She can also carve a really good Sunday roast, although this rarely proves useful in her battles with Kaos.

Stealth Elf isn't the only master of stealth around here, though. I can be pretty sneaky, too, when I want to be. That's how I managed to get my hands on Stealth Elf's old notebook, where she jotted down her mentor's words of ninja wisdom.

These secrets have remained hidden for centuries, only being passed from master to pupil. It can't do any harm to have a quick peek, though. Let's be quick, before Stealth Elf discovers her notebook is missing . . .

THE FOREST GUARDIAN'S NINJA WISDOM

"Fear. Doubt. Squeaky shoes. These are the enemies of the true ninja."

"The shadows are your friends. But don't lend them money; they'll never give it back."

"A ninja's greatest weapon is stealth. Failing that, you can't go wrong with a big sword."

"To be truly silent, the ninja must become the very essence of silence itself. Also: Never eat baked beans."

"Sometimes the best hiding place is in plain sight. But more often it is behind a tree."

"Distraction is an important skill in the . . . WOW, LOOK OVER THERE—FLYING SHEEP!"

NINJA CLOTHING

Appropriate ninja clothing choices:
- Black leather
- Gray leather
- Dark brown leather

Inappropriate ninja clothing choices:
- Yellow nylon
- An orange dress with pink polka dots on it
- An orange dress with any other color of polka dots on it
- An electric-blue leotard
- A hat with bells on it
- Anything made from gold-colored satin
- Glow-in-the-dark socks
- Anything with a colorful target embroidered over the heart
- Roller skates

HOW TO BE STEALTHY

1. Don't make any noise.
2. Er . . . that's it, really.

DROPPING IN ON THE
TROLLVERINES

FLYNN'S FABLES

There's nothing I like more than ballooning around Skylands and watching the folks below. Once, Stump Smash asked if he could come along with me. I told him he could —because I'm a nice guy like that—and we set off sailing through the sky.

Now, I think it must've been something to do with the extra weight because, well, we crashed. It wasn't my fault. One minute we were cruising along, the next someone goes and puts a mountain right in our path. How was I to know that was going to happen?

I've crashed a few times over the years, so the crashing itself wasn't too much of a problem. The problem was, we landed right in the middle of a Trollverine pack, and those guys did not look happy!

I think it must've been something about the sight of the Trollverines' blades (maybe they reminded him of the blades the trolls had used to chop down his forest) but something just snapped inside old Stump Smash. He started swinging with his big mallet fists, sending Trollverine after Trollverine flipping way up into the air.

When those guys were airborne, Stump Smash swung and—THWACK!—off they flew, before smashing head-first into the mountain (see, they didn't notice it either!).

Still, Stump Smash was heavily outnumbered, so I did the only thing I could do—I created a diversion! It may have looked like I was just running away, but I was definitely creating a diversion. Some of the Trollverines came after me, but I can run fast when I want to—and I really wanted to, if you know what I mean!

I shook them off and kept running until I heard voices. I ran in the direction of the sound, crying out for help (or just crying—Hugo). Imagine my shock when I ran straight into . . . Stump Smash!

Somehow I'd managed to go around in a complete circle and arrive back where I'd started. I was about to run away again —to get help—when I realized the Trollverines were slumped unconscious all over the place. That Stumpy dude had really gotten into the swing of things

and taken down the whole lot of them single-handed! Or single-malleted, or whatever.

We managed to get the balloon back into the air and headed for home, but now Stump Smash insists on coming out with me at least once a week, in the hope we crash-land into another pack of Trollverines! That tree dude is barking mad! Get it? Barking! Like *tree bark*! Sometimes I crack me up.

CAMO'S GARDENING TIPS

Camo might not have green fingers, but he makes up for it by being green pretty much everywhere else! As a half-dragon, half-plant born in the shade of the Tree of Life, he possesses the unique ability to, er, grow plants quickly. As Master Eon's chief weed-puller and hedge-trimmer, here are some of his top tips for keeping your yard in order . . .

1. WEED OUT THE TROLLS

Even the nicest garden can lose its charm if a dozen trolls start messing around in it. Get rid of them—quick! There are many different ways of clearing them out. Explosive fireballs are my favorite.

2. WATER REGULARLY

It's a lot of work during dry weather keeping Master Eon's garden watered. One shortcut is to invite over Gill Grunt, then pick a fight with him. When he attacks with his water cannon, run around the garden as fast as you can, and the plants will get a cool, refreshing drink.

3. DON'T LET TREES AND HEDGES GROW OUT OF CONTROL

It's important to keep bushes and other foliage neatly trimmed, or you'll soon have a jungle on your hands. It's a good idea to invite friends to help you with the chopping. A word of warning though: Don't invite Boomer, unless you want your trees "trimmed" into a million burning pieces.

4. WANT TO ENJOY YOUR GARDEN AT NIGHT?

Grab some flame imps and tie them to poles, then place the poles in the soil. The imps will not only provide light—they'll help keep you warm, too. Warning: They may also try to attack you.

5. A ROCKERY CAN BE A GREAT FEATURE IN ANY GARDEN

Whenever the Skylanders defeat a rock walker, I get them to bring it to Master Eon's garden and pile it up in the corner. There are over two hundred rock walkers piled up there, and Master Eon's rockery now closely resembles a mountain.

GARDENING PRANKS

If there's one thing I love more than gardening, it's playing pranks. It's even better when I can combine the two. I don't want to give away too many of my secrets, so here are the names of only my favorite gardening pranks.

1. The Exploding Carrot
2. The Rake in the Face
3. Chainsaw Surprise
4. LOOK OUT—Shed!
5. Toxic Grass

6. The Rusty Hinge
7. Beware of the Frog
8. Down the Mud Hole
9. Wheelbarrow Face
10. Timber Splat

HUGO'S NOTES

FOREST BESTIARY

Along with the Skylanders, there are lots of other creatures in Skylands associated with the Life Element. Many of those live deep in the forests. Some are pure of nature, others stray along darker paths. All of them smell faintly of wet grass. Let's meet a few of them . . .

ARBO

I am reliably informed (by Arbo himself) that Arbo is the son of Barbo and a child of Larbo. Unfortunately, no one has any idea who either of these people are. Arbo, though, is a more-or-less-helpful tree creature with the ability to make plants grow to immense size. When I first met Arbo, he was only a few seconds old, and yet somehow had memories as old as Skylands itself. Very strange.

CORN HORNETS

These nasty little bugs can be found in most forests, their striped bodies zipping around and their dragonlike wings beating furiously. A sting from a corn hornet can stun even the hardiest Skylander, so it's best to avoid them at all costs. If you do ever find yourself stung by a corn hornet, the pain can be eased by applying banana gravy directly to the affected area, and crying uncontrollably for several hours.

LUMBERJACK TROLLS

With the exception of the Skylander Boomer, there's no such thing as a nice troll. Lumberjack trolls are among the worst of the lot, though. They live only to chop down forests, destroying whole woodlands in order to make weapons for the armies of Kaos. They got a real shock when they chopped down Stump Smash's forest, though . . . as well as some severe concussions and a few broken bones.

LIFE SPELL PUNKS

It's hard enough battling enemies without Life Spell Punks getting in the way. These annoying magic-makers help to heal the forces of Kaos, meaning Skylanders have to work even harder to secure victory. Luckily, the Spell Punks themselves aren't particularly tough. One good whack to their silly hats takes care of them and, once they're out of the way, fighting the meaner bad guys gets a lot easier.

NINJA TRAINING HAS ITS USES

Stealth Elf has no memory of her childhood. Like, none at all. I'm pretty forgetful sometimes, but she doesn't remember anything! Her first memory is of waking up in a hollow tree, although she has a vague recollection that she may have been dreaming of stampeding sheep before then.

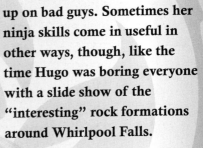

FLYNN'S FABLES

The Forest Guardian found her and trained her to do all that cool ninja stuff she can do, like nifty acrobatics and sneaking up on bad guys. Sometimes her ninja skills come in useful in other ways, though, like the time Hugo was boring everyone with a slide show of the "interesting" rock formations around Whirlpool Falls.

He'd gathered us all in one place by pretending he had some really important news to share. Next thing we know, he's locked the doors and we're stuck looking at pictures of boulders. He said they were "fascinating specimens," but they just looked like boring old rocks to me. Everyone was yawning and complaining, but he didn't

pay any attention. He just kept showing us those slides. The only person in the room who looked interested was Stealth Elf. She sat near the front, staring up at the screen and paying attention to every slide that went past.

She's not usually the patient type, but she seemed to be totally gripped by those rock photos. The rest of us moaned and groaned our way through it until Hugo finally let us out.

We all made a mad dash for the exit, and who did we see enjoying the fresh air outside? Stealth Elf! It turned out she'd snuck away the moment she saw Hugo bringing out his projector, and left one of her duplicates behind to watch the show. She'd been outside the whole time while the rest of us learned about why a pointy rock was more interesting than a bumpy one.

I don't know how the Forest Guardian would feel about her using her ninja skills for something like that, but I know one thing—every single Skylander there wished that they'd been able to do the same thing!

LIFE:
ELEMENTS UNITE

The Elements that make up the Core of Light interact with one another in some really cool ways, and Life is no exception. Without Life, where would we be? (Dead, probably—Flynn)

WEAKNESS

The Undead Element is a real threat to Life. The dark, creeping shadows of the Undead sap the Life energy from everything they touch, leaving them withered and frail.

HOW LIFE ENTWINES WITH THE OTHER ELEMENTS

AIR
The spores of Life are carried far and wide on the wind

EARTH
Life's seeds bring dense foliage from the Earth

UNDEAD
Breathes new Life into the Undead

FIRE
Provides fuel for Fire's flames

MAGIC
Helps ancient Magic strengthen and grow

TECH
Adds new branches to Tech development

WATER
Uses Water's nourishment to grow to great heights

LIFE
SKYLANDERS

CAMO

ZOOK

STUMP SMASH

STEALTH ELF

SHROOMBOOM

TREE REX

42

UNDEAD
SKYLANDERS

HEX

FRIGHT RIDER

CYNDER

CHOP CHOP

EYE-BRAWL

GHOST ROASTER

WHERE DOES UNDEAD COME FROM?

Many think there's something creepy about the Undead Element. That's probably because those empowered by it are often skeletal, ghoulish creatures.

I'll be honest—they used to give me the heebie-jeebies. But that was before I realized that most of them are just like the rest of us, only, er, not technically alive.

Most Undead creatures come from the Underworld, a dark place that would be absolutely terrifying if it wasn't for the delicious pies.

Many creatures—including some Skylanders —have been changed forever as a result of visiting the Underworld. Some have found their very souls twisted beyond recognition. Others, such as Cynder, simply like hanging out in graveyards. But all have it within themselves to use their Undead abilities for good.

The Undead Element inhabits the darkest corners of Skylands, lurking in the shadows, ready to pounce— and then serve up a lovely snack or tell a terrible joke.

IN THE UNDERWORLD, GRUESOME GHOULS LURK AROUND EVERY CORNER.

LAND OF THE UNDEAD DOS AND DON'TS

Despite its reputation as a truly horrible and frightening place, some people insist on visiting the Land of the Undead in order to see what all the fuss is about. While I advise strongly against it, if you do decide to venture into this dark realm, here are some things you should and shouldn't do.

DO
kiss your loved ones good-bye before you set off.

DO
change your mind at the last minute and stay at home instead.

DON'T
make plans for after you return. You almost certainly won't.

DON'T
forget to make a will.

DON'T
sell your eternal soul to strangers, no matter how much they offer.

DO
bring a change of underwear. It's a frightening place.

46

DO

visit the
gift shop.

DON'T

look the shop assistant
in the eye, ask him what
anything costs, or show
him anything yellow.

DO

wear running
shoes.

DON'T

say "Ugh, it stinks
down here,"
in a loud voice.

DO

try the pizza.
Flynn assures
me it's delicious.

DON'T

take Flynn's word
on anything. That's
good advice anytime.

GHOUL WATCH!

Is there anything more terrifying than a ghost? Well, yes. Quite a few things, probably. A really angry cyclops for one. (Or a massive dragon— Flynn). Yes, or a massive dragon—thank you, Flynn.

But ghosts are still very scary indeed, and should be avoided at all costs. Ghost World is obviously full of them, as is Ghost Roaster's kitchen after he's just received a delivery. But they can be found in other places, too. So, how do you tell when a ghost is in the vicinity? Fortunately for you, I've prepared this guide to help you out.

IS YOUR HOUSE HAUNTED?

The following are clues that your house may be haunted:

1. It's very cold. Watch out— there may be a ghost nearby. Or someone's left the fridge open.

2. Your toys vanish when you're not around. Is it a horrible poltergeist, or has your little brother been sneaking into your room when you're not looking?

3. You hear terrifying noises during the night. Is there an evil specter outside your bedroom door, or is your dad just snoring again?

4. A ghost floats through your bedroom wall and shouts "Boo!" This is a strong sign that your house may well be haunted. It is vital you take approprIate action.

HOW TO DEAL WITH GHOSTS

Ghosts come in all shapes and sizes, and it's important to learn how to deal with them. Here's what to do if confronted by one of the ghosts listed below.

SPECTER:
Run away.

SPOOK:
Run away.

POLTERGEIST:
Run away very fast.

GHOUL:
Scream.
Then run away.

PHANTOM:
Scream. Faint.
Wake up several
minutes later. Run away.

FLESH-DEVOURING SOUL-SUCKER
Die of fright. Then run away.

ENTER AT YOUR PERIL!

EYE-BRAWL

100%

UNDEAD RATING

DID YOU KNOW?

As well as being impossible to beat in a staring competition—on account of not being able to blink —Eye-Brawl has a real talent for hide-and-seek. His towering height and penetrating gaze allow him to quickly spot even the most well-camouflaged opponent. Things become more difficult for him when it's his turn to hide, though, as it's virtually impossible for him to squeeze into the cupboard under the stairs.

FACT FILE

● Was once two separate beings—a floating eyeball and a headless giant

● The two combined their strength after duelling for a century

● It's said that if Eye-Brawl ever cries, entire villages will get washed away

● Undisputed Skylands staring-contest champion

FRIGHT RIDER

DID YOU KNOW?

Before becoming one of the Undead, Fright was terrified of pretty much everything. His list of fears included shadows, curtains, certain sandwiches and having a jousting spear accidentally plunged into his head. All that changed when he munched on a bag of skele-oats so that he could be transformed into a skeleton and rescue Rider. Now he isn't scared of much, apart from getting a spear through his skull. And of sandwiches.

FACT FILE

- An unstoppable team—the elf, Rider, and his skeletal ostrich, Fright
- Jousting champions for three years running
- Rider was banished to the Underworld by a jealous competitor
- Fright bravely sacrificed himself to save his friend

UNDEAD RATING

 68%

51

HEX

FACT FILE

- Perhaps the most powerful sorceress in history
- Was hunted by the Undead Dragon King, Malefor
- Joined the ranks of the unliving to defeat Malefor and protect her fellow sorcerers
- Looks terrifying, but is dedicated to the forces of good

DID YOU KNOW?

Because of her appearance, many people are scared of Hex, fearing she will use her magic for evil purposes. In an attempt to set their minds at ease, Hex once swapped her dark robes for a frilly pink dress with yellow polka dots. If anything, this made her look even more alarming, and—to everyone's relief—she quickly changed back.

UNDEAD RATING

CYNDER

FACT FILE

- Egg-napped by the evil Malefor before she had hatched
- Brainwashed and trained in the ways of evil and darkness
- Menaced Skylands until defeated by Spyro himself
- Now fighting for good ... most of the time.

65%

DID YOU KNOW?

Darkness still lurks within Cynder, and most Skylanders try to keep out of her way just to be on the safe side. Wrecking Ball once thought it would be funny to trip her up with his long tongue. He soon regretted it when Cynder zapped the tongue with her Spectral Lightning. Poor Wrecking Ball couldn't eat properly for two weeks.

UNDEAD RATING

CHOP CHOP

FACT FILE

- Created by the ancient Arkeyans
- Wields a sword and shield of indestructible metal
- A fusion of Undead and Tech Elements
- Can grow spiky bones from the ground to attack enemies

DID YOU KNOW?

Chop Chop may be an ancient skeletal warrior created by the Arkeyans, but he's not without his fun side. Every winter, when he isn't using his mighty shield to protect Skylands, he uses it to take local Skylands children sledging. It's possible that many of them even enjoy it, although the way they scream makes it hard to tell.

UNDEAD RATING

GHOST ROASTER

DID YOU KNOW?

Before being turned into a terrifying Undead ghost-muncher, Ghost Roaster was one of the best chefs in all of Skylands. He still likes to cook, but many of his recipes are not as appetizing as they once were. His poached heads are particularly unpleasant, while his eyeball surprise should be avoided at all costs.

57%

UNDEAD RATING

FACT FILE

- Loves to eat. And eat. And eat
- Was once a mild-mannered chef, until he stumbled into the Valley of the Undead
- Doomed to carry a rattling ball and chain forever
- Knows a hundred and one recipes for cooking ghosts

SECRETS OF THE ELEMENTS:
UNDEAD

Of all the Elements, none hold as many secrets as the shadowy Undead. We shall never be able to solve all its riddles and enigmas but, through many years of research, I have unraveled at least a few of its many mysteries.

UNDEAD GATES

When accessing their Elemental gates, most Skylanders build a bridge to allow them to pass through. Undead Skylanders are no exception, but their bridges are formed from the bones of their fallen enemies. It's even worse than it sounds when you see it up close.

YOU CAN'T HELP BUT ADMIRE THE UNDEAD'S ABILITY TO KEEP FINDING NEW USES FOR DISCARDED BONES.

ANCIENT GUARDIANS

The Arkeyans built weapons of tremendous power, capable of destroying entire islands in one fell swoop. Scared that these weapons might fall into the wrong hands, the Arkeyans merged Undead magic and technology to create their Elite Guard. Highly advanced and utterly terrifying at the same time, no one dared challenge the Elite Guard, and the Arkeyan

weapons remained safe for generations as a result.

EVIL UNDEAD DOUBLES

In his quest to conquer Skylands, Kaos devises all sorts of tricks. One of his plans involved creating duplicates of all the Skylanders—evil duplicates! Because of the dark magic

already flowing through them, the evil duplicates of the Undead Skylanders are particularly nasty. Chop Chop, Hex, and Ghost Roaster all have evil doubles out there somewhere. Fortunately, the heroic originals are more than a match for them!

CALI'S HEROIC CHALLENGES

Some of those Undead Skylanders are pretty scary dudes. It takes real guts to even look at them, never mind give them challenges. Luckily, my Cali has got plenty of guts, and I bet they're the cutest, prettiest little guts anyone has ever had! (That's just weird—Hugo).

ZOMBIE
DANCE PARTY

Not all zombies are flesh-eating monsters who want to eat your face off—some of them just love to dance. When a group of dancing zombies had their heads stolen by Spell Punks, Cali decided Cynder should get them back. I'm a big fan of my Cali, but sometimes I do wonder where she gets her ideas from. Cynder was sent to a dungeon filled with traps, Chompies, and other little nasties and had to track down six missing zombie heads. Once the dragon put them back together, the zombies showed off some of their moves. Those guys think they can really dance, but personally I thought they were rotten!

DELIVERY DAY

Delivery Day is one of my favorite days of the year —a day when each of us gives and receives a special gift. Cali challenged Fright Rider to do the deliveries this year. It sounded easy, but with enemies swarming all around him and a tight time limit, old Frighty only just managed to make it through the challenge and get everyone's gifts delivered. In case you're wondering, my Delivery Day gift was a large diamond from Clam-Tron 4000. In return, I gave General Robot a cheeseburger. Well, it's the thought that counts! Man, I sure miss that burger, though . . .

FLYNN'S FABLES

DINNER
FOR
TWO

A few weeks ago Cali and I had a special anniversary. It was exactly one year since she first put me in a headlock, and I wanted to celebrate in style. I decided to cook us a romantic meal, which would've been great—but cooking isn't exactly my strong point. I'm more of a rugged–outdoors type.

I asked Ghost Roaster to help out, partly because he used to be a world-class chef, but mostly because he offered to do it for free. I set the table and created some mood lighting with a few Flame Imps, and we sat down to a delicious meal.

At least, that was the plan. Our first clue that there was something wrong with dinner was when it started to crawl away. Cali managed to tackle our meal before it could make it outside, but neither of us felt like eating it after that.

It said "thanks," then ran away, trailing gravy all over the floor.

Still, I wasn't going to let that spoil our anniversary, so I asked Ghost Roaster to bring out the cheesecake I'd asked him to make. Old Ghostie's face fell and he gave an embarrassed little cough. Turned out he thought I'd said "knees-cake," and he'd baked us a cake with knees in it. I don't know whose knees they were, and I didn't ask. The evening was already turning into a disaster, and I didn't want to make it any worse.

I'll say one thing, though—Ghost Roaster knows his stuff! The cake was absolutely delicious (although a bit knobby in parts). For some reason, Cali didn't want any, so I ate the whole lot myself. Then I immediately fell asleep, like I always do after a big meal. Cali woke me up by putting me in another headlock— it was the most romantic moment of my life!

And the most painful.

ELEMENTAL GATES: UNDEAD LOCATIONS

You know I said earlier that there are hidden areas around Skylands that are only open to Life Skylanders? Well, guess what —the Undead Element has them, too! Here are my observations on those encountered by the Undead Skylanders during their quest to rebuild the Core of Light . . .

SKY SCHOONER DOCKS

Near the beginning of this area you'll use a big gun to shoot down some flying zeppelin balloons. Once you've done that, head through the gate and you'll encounter a Drow Witch. She'll throw energy discs at you—trust me, you don't want to be hit by any of those! Once you've beaten her, continue along the wooden walkway and you'll find the Elemental gate. It's easy to find, but things are not so easy once you're through it. Watch out for the spinning propellers, and use those bounce pads wisely!

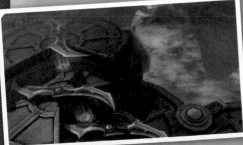

DIFFICULTY

EASY

HARD

BATTLEFIELD

HARD

DIFFICULTY

EASY

Finding this Undead Elemental gate is hard work, but it's worth it! In the Defensive Perimeter area of Battlefield, work your way along the trenches and through the gates until you reach a teleporter located beside a defensive wall. Using the teleporter will take you to a cannon mounted high on a rampart. Defeat the guard and use the cannon to knock a hole in the defensive wall. Teleport back, pop through the hole you shot, then follow the path on the left until you find another cannon at the top of some stone steps. You'll find the gate there, too. The challenges that await you beyond the gate are tricky indeed. Be patient, and you'll earn a special reward.

CRAWLING CATACOMBS

HARD

DIFFICULTY

EASY

In the Alchemy Lab area seek out the three keys. Once you've found the third key and unlocked the last gate, the lights will go out and visibility will be very limited. Calm your nerves, Portal Master! Head left and you'll find the Elemental gate. That's the good news. The bad news is that it's surrounded by Spider Spitters. You'll have to take care of them if you want to get through. Beyond the gate you'll find an area known as the Chamber of Eyes. Solve the puzzle within and claim your prize!

PUTTING
A SMILE ON HEX'S FACE

FLYNN'S FABLES

Since being changed into a spooky Undead sorceress, Hex has seemed a little down in the dumps. She always looks unhappy—even when I tell her my jokes. In fact, especially when I tell her my jokes.

A while back, some of the guys got together to see if they could make Hex smile. It was a tough challenge, but there was no shortage of Skylanders willing to give it a try.

First up, Camo exploded a melon in Hex's face. I thought it was hysterical, but Hex didn't see the funny side. Nor did Camo after she trapped him in a bone fortress. Luckily, she let him out later.

Zap used his electric abilities to make lightning bolts in the shape of Hex's name appear in the air. She wasn't impressed. Slam Bam juggled snowballs, Stump Smash played the drums —even Hugo tried to cheer her up by putting on some silly glasses. (Hey, those are my normal glasses! – Hugo) None of it worked, though.

end. The big yeti fell face-first into his snowballs. That did the job! As Slam Bam hopped around clutching his backside and spluttering out mouthfuls of snow, Hex burst out laughing. It only lasted a second, and then she went back to looking all scary and brooding again, but everyone saw it. Well, everyone except Trigger Happy, who was too busy running away to notice.

No matter what anyone tried, Hex remained stone-faced. Not as stone-faced as Bash, obviously, whose face looks a bit like it could actually be made of stone, but stone-faced all the same.

It looked like nothing was going to cheer up Hex, so everyone started to drift home. But all was not lost! As Slam Bam was bending over to pick up his snowballs, Trigger Happy "accidentally" fired one of his guns. A gold coin shot out and hit Slam Bam right on the rear

T-BONE'S GRUESOME GAGS

Most Undead life forms are brooding, miserable types. However, there is one who is just the opposite. The skeleton T-Bone enjoys nothing more than a good joke. Unfortunately, he doesn't know any good jokes, so we're forced to put up with his awful ones instead.

He asked me if he could share some of his gags here in this book. I, of course, said no. Sadly, he wouldn't take that for an answer, and I finally gave in. I hope you can forgive me—some of the jokes below are real stinkers.

Q. What musical instrument do skeletons play?
A. The trom-BONE!

Q. What's Cynder's favorite day of the week?
A. FRIGHT-day!

Q. Why are graveyards so noisy?
A. Because of all the *coffin*!

Q. Why are vampires so unpopular?
A. Because they're a real pain in the neck!

Q. How do Undead Elementals tell the future?
A. They read their HORROR-scopes!

Q. What do you get if you cross Slam Bam with a vampire?
A. Frostbite!

Q. What's Ghost Roaster's favorite dessert?
A. Ice SCREAM!

Q. Where do baby Undead Elementals go during the day?
A. The day-scare center!

Q. What's Hex's favorite amusement-park ride?
A. The roller *ghoster*!

Q. How do Undead Elementals like their eggs?
A. Terri-*fried*!

A BONE TO PICK WITH
CHOP CHOP

FLYNN'S FABLES

Did you hear about the time Chop Chop fought off a troll invasion using just his head? He didn't do it on purpose—it was just that Hot Dog didn't leave him much choice.

That sneaky Fire pup thought it'd be funny to nab Chop Chop's bony arms and legs while he was sleeping, and bury them somewhere in Master Eon's garden. Unfortunately, Hot Dog's memory isn't great, and when Chop Chop woke up looking for his missing limbs, the flame pooch couldn't remember where he'd buried them. The other Skylanders all pitched in to help and soon we were all digging holes in Master Eon's garden (Camo wasn't happy about that one little bit). We were so busy digging that most of us didn't notice a whole gang of trolls come strolling past!

Luckily, Chop Chop did. The trolls must've thought he'd be easy to defeat without any arms or legs, but they didn't count on Chop Chop's determination. Or his Arkeyan tech helmet, for that matter.

Choppy started bouncing around like a jack-in-the-box, head-butting anything that moved. The trolls tried to stand their ground, but it's not easy when the armored torso of a living skeleton is flinging itself at you over and over again.

The clanking of metal and the screaming of the trolls brought me and the Skylanders running over. I think the trolls were relieved to see us, to be honest, because it meant Chop Chop stopped attacking long enough for them to run away. Hot Dog eventually remembered where he'd hidden Chop Chop's bones. They were behind a hedge, and not buried in Master Eon's garden at all. Everyone got a little annoyed about that, but it's impossible to stay mad at Hot Dog for long. He's so adorable—just like me!

THE DARK DRAGONESS

Before being recruited by Master Eon into the ranks of the Skylanders, Cynder was feared in almost every corner of the world.

Kidnapped as an egg by the Undead Dragon King, Malefor, Cynder was raised to serve the forces of evil. As she grew, the dark power of the Undead granted her incredible abilities, which she used to terrorize innocent people.

Whole villages fell beneath her mystical lightning attacks, and even the bravest warriors would turn and flee when they saw her swooping down from the clouds with her talons outstretched.

Twisted and corrupted by evil, Cynder was Malefor's black-hearted harbringer of misery and despair. But Spyro believed there was good in her, deep down. (Waaaay deep down—Flynn.)

When he confronted her, a ferocious battle ensued. Despite Cynder's dark powers, Spyro was able to defeat her. When he did, Malefor's control over her was broken. No longer was she the puppet of the Undead Dragon King, and she was determined to make amends for all the suffering she had caused while under his control.

Realizing how much she had changed, Master Eon recruited her into the Skylanders. Although she now fights for good, she still struggles with her dark side from time to time. Most of her fellow Skylanders try to keep out of her way—just in case her inner darkness takes over once more.

MALEFOR, THE UNDEAD DRAGON KING

There are plenty of nasty things lurking in the Underworld, but Malefor was perhaps the nastiest of all. For centuries, Malefor lay down there in the shadows, sending his dark minions up to the world above to carry out his bidding.

No one knows where the Undead Dragon King came from, but everyone knows where he went —up in smoke. That's what he gets for trying to imprison Hex. Dragon King or not, it's never wise to mess with an angry sorceress.

Many people believe that Malefor will one day return, but if he does Hex will be waiting for him—with her fellow Skylanders standing by her side.

TOPSY-TURVY JOUSTING

FLYNN'S FABLES

You all know that Fright Rider used to be a champion jousting team, right, back before their Skylanders days? Fright the Ostrich was a blindingly fast runner, and Rider had a perfect aim with that jousting spear of his. They were pretty much unbeatable together.

But did you know their first-ever tournament almost ended in total disaster? It was only some quick thinking from Rider that saved the day.

The tournament had been going well. Fright and Rider had battled through the early rounds and managed to secure themselves a place in the final. They were really excited—this was the first time they'd ever taken part in a real jousting competition, and they were one bout away from winning.

That was when disaster struck. Their opponent "accidentally" dropped his spear onto Fright's foot, hurting it badly. The poor ostrich could barely walk, never mind run. The judges, who hadn't seen a thing, announced that if Fright couldn't compete, then the match would be forfeited and their sneaky opponent would win.

Rider was having none of that, though. The rules said teams had to be made up of one steed and one rider, but they didn't say which one had to do the carrying and which had to hold the spear.

Quick as a flash, Rider lifted Fright up onto his back, and they were back in the game! Rider couldn't run as fast as Fright, of course, and Fright wasn't as accurate with the jousting spear, but they were both determined to win.

In front of a cheering crowd, Fright and Rider knocked that sneaky cheat right off his steed and into the mud. It was the first time the pair had won a tournament—but it definitely wasn't the last. Although when Fright's foot healed, he went back to carrying Rider instead of the other way around!

GHOST ROASTER'S DEAD GOOD MEALS

Before joining the ranks of the Undead, Ghost Roaster was a brilliant chef named Olav. The people of his village worshipped his cooking skills and would line up overnight to try his latest delicacy.

Very few people line up to taste his food these days, though. Perhaps the recipes he shares with us below will explain why.

PICKLED SPOOK SLIME

Ingredients:

1 bucket of ghostly ectoplasm
3 litres of strong vinegar
A pinch of salt to taste

Method

1. Form ectoplasm into gooey balls. No special tools are required for this—just stick your hands in, right up to the elbow.
2. Drop slime balls into a jar. A clean one, ideally, but dirty will do.
3. Cover balls with vinegar. Add salt if required.
4. Place lid on jar.
5. Store in a darkened room for six hundred years.
6 Eat.

SPA-GHOSTIE BOLOGNAISE

Ingredients:

1 ghost (evil), finely chopped
1 other ghost (evil), minced
1 more ghost (evil), rolled flat
1 jar bolognaise sauce (good or evil, it doesn't matter)

ICE SCREAM

Ingredients:

1 litre double cream
3 drops vanilla essence
1 terror-stricken scream of a frightened child

Method

1. In a frying pan, cook the minced ghost until it is lightly browned.
2. Add the finely chopped ghost and the bolognaise sauce, then allow to simmer.
3. Meanwhile, force the flat ghost through a pasta maker. You should be left with long, thin ghostly strands.
4. Boil the ghostly strands for four minutes.
5. Serve with a chunk of garlic bread. Unless you're a vampire, in which case you should probably leave the bread.

Method

1. First, get the scream. There are many ways to do this. My favorite involves hiding in a bedroom cupboard until the child is just about to fall asleep, then leaping out and shouting "WAAAAAAGH!" at the top of my voice. Remember to have an enchanted bottle ready with which to catch the scream.
2. Combine all three ingredients in a large bowl.
3. Place bowl in freezer.
4. Hide from child's angry parents for several hours.
5. Eat! The ice scream, I mean, not the parents.

UNDEAD:
ELEMENTS UNITE

Despite its dark origins, the Undead Element is a vital part of the Core of Light. It combines with the other Elements in some unusual—and unexpected—ways.

WEAKNESS

While the Undead Element is strong against the Life Element, it is at the mercy of Magic. Spells and sorcery really take their toll, and Undead Elementals should beware the wrath of wizards.

HOW UNDEAD ENTWINES WITH THE OTHER ELEMENTS

AIR
The stench of the Undead creeps like fog on the breeze

EARTH
Undead can spread its rotten touch through the soil

FIRE
Adds choking black smoke to the flames

LIFE
Draws strength from the Life force, draining it dry

MAGIC
Twists magical forces for its own dark ends

TECH
Fuses with Tech to create Elite Guard warriors

WATER
Turns clear flowing pools into dark, stagnant ponds

FAREWELL!

Well, I don't know about you, but my brain is fried after all that, and it takes a lot to fry a brain this size. So much information! Some of it is exciting and thrilling, and yet at the same time useful (mine), some of it is dull enough to make your eyes pop out and roll out of the room (Hugo's). I hope your eyes stay in place long enough to read this last part: Farewell, my friend, and good luck in your battles against the forces of Kaos!

In order to fry your brain you need to possess a brain to begin with, so Flynn should be absolutely fine. His flights of fancy may make for amusing reading, but when it comes to imparting knowledge that will aid you in your heroic endeavors, we all know who you should turn to (hint: me). I hope the wisdom I have shared on these pages will help you become a more skilled Portal Master, and I believe that Skylands can rest easier with you to help protect it.

UNTIL NEXT TIME, PORTAL MASTER!